# RAINFORESTS

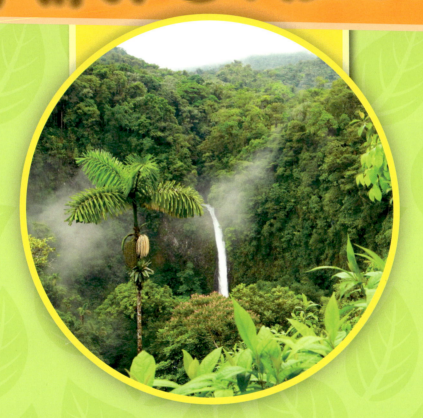

Mary-Jane Wilkins

**W**

# FRANKLIN WATTS
LONDON • SYDNEY

Franklin Watts
First published in Great Britain in 2016 by
The Watts Publishing Group

For Brown Bear Books Ltd:
Picture Researcher: Clare Newman
Designer: Melissa Roskell
Design Manager: Keith Davis
Editorial Director: Lindsey Lowe
Children's Publisher: Anne O'Daly

ISBN 978 1 4451 5171 7

Printed in China

Franklin Watts
An imprint of
Hachette Children's Group
Part of The Watts Publishing Group
Carmelite House
50 Victoria Embankment
London EC4Y 0DZ

An Hachette UK company
www.hachette.co.uk

www.franklinwatts.co.uk

# CONTENTS

# Where do RAINFORESTS GROW?

Tropical rainforests grow where the weather is hot and very rainy. They grow in countries near the Equator. This is the imaginary line that runs around the middle of the Earth.

Leafcutter ants can carry more than 50 times their own body weight.

## WOW!

The biggest rainforest in the world is the **Amazon** in South America. At least **2.5 million** types of plants and animals live there.

Equator

rainforest

South America

About half of the animals in the world live in rainforests. Many live high in the treetops because that is where they find their food. You can find out about some rainforest animals in this book.

# FROGS

Many different frogs live in rainforests. Some are brightly coloured – red, blue or green. Flying frogs spread out their webbed feet to **glide** between trees.

This is a poison dart frog. It has poison in its skin.

Flying frogs have big pads on their toes that help them stick to trees when they land. They eat insects.

# TREE KANGAROO

Tree kangaroos live high in the rainforests of New Guinea and Australia.

A baby is called a joey. When it is born it climbs into its mother's pouch. It lives there for the first months of its life.

These animals have long tails and strong arms. Their curved claws help them climb trees. They can **jump** a **long** way from trees to the ground – up to 18 m.

# SLOTH

Sloths are slow-moving animals. They spend the days sleeping. They wake up at night and eat leaves, fruit and buds. Then they go to sleep again.

Sloths often sleep for 10 hours at a time.

Most sloths are the same size as a small dog. Their strong front legs and long claws help them hang from trees.

Baby sloths are born in trees while their mother hangs upside down!

# ORANGUTAN

These large orange apes have very **long** arms. They can be 2 m from fingertip to fingertip.

Orangutans make leafy nests to sleep in. They use big leaves as umbrellas.

A mother looks after her baby for six or seven years.

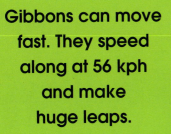

Gibbons can move fast. They speed along at 56 kph and make huge leaps.

# GIBBON

Gibbons are the acrobats of the rainforest. They **swing** through the trees, gripping branches with long, strong hands.

# JAGUAR

The jaguar is the **biggest** cat in South America. It is a predator. The markings on its coat help it hide among the plants and shadows of the rainforest, as it hunts other animals.

The markings on a jaguar's coat are called rosettes.

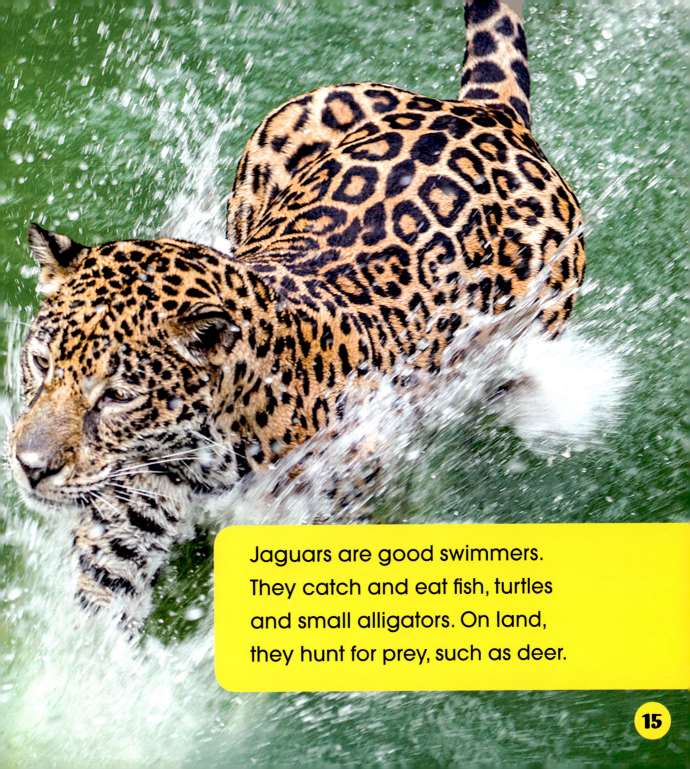

Jaguars are good swimmers. They catch and eat fish, turtles and small alligators. On land, they hunt for prey, such as deer.

# AYE-AYE

The small aye-aye lives in the rainforests of Madagascar. It sleeps most of the day.

These animals have big ears and thin fingers.

Aye-ayes use their **l o n g** middle finger to hook grubs to eat from under the bark of trees.

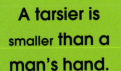

A tarsier is smaller than a man's hand.

# TARSIER

The tarsier is a tiny animal with **huge** eyes. The eyes help it to hunt at night. It cannot move its eyes, but it can turn its head to face backwards.

# CHIMPANZEE

Chimpanzees live in big groups in African rainforests. They stand and walk upright, or walk on all fours. They also **swing** through the trees on long arms.

Baby chimps stay with their mother for six years.

Chimps use sticks to dig grubs out of logs to eat. They also smash open nuts with stones. They sleep in nests that they make from leaves and branches.

# TAPIR

Tapirs are **big** animals like pigs.

They love water and wallowing in mud.

## WOW!

A tapir pulls fruit and leaves off trees with its short, bendy trunk.

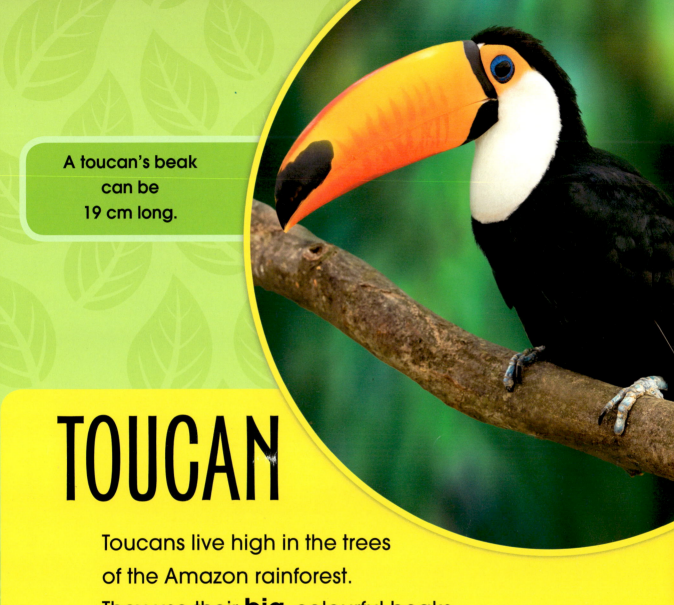

A toucan's beak
can be
19 cm long.

# TOUCAN

Toucans live high in the trees
of the Amazon rainforest.
They use their **big**, colourful beaks
to pick fruit and catch insects to eat.

# RAINFOREST FACTS

 There are two types of rainforest. The tropical ones are always hot. Temperate rainforests are cool in winter and hot in summer.

 Rainforests are getting smaller. People are cutting them down. They use the wood from the trees and plant crops or build roads on the land.

 Rainforests are very wet. Around 198 cm of rain fall on them every year.

 Tropical rainforests can be about 27°Celsius in the day and almost as hot at night.

# USEFUL WORDS

**Equator**
The imaginary line around the middle of the Earth. Countries near the Equator are very hot.

**glide**
To move smoothly.

**predator**
An animal that hunts and kills other animals for food. The jaguar is a predator. ➡

**prey**
An animal hunted and eaten by another animal. Deer are the prey of a jaguar.

# FIND OUT MORE

*Eyewonder: Rainforest,* Dorling Kindersley, 2013.

*Orangutan,* Anita Ganeri, Raintree, 2010.

*Rainforest (Leapfrog Learners),* Annabelle Lynch, Franklin Watts, 2014.

*Up Close: Rainforest,* Paul Harrison, Franklin Watts, 2011.

# INDEX